Hunted in Hong Kong

I Talk You Talk Press

CONTENTS

CHAPTER ONE

Rose Chen looked out of the window in the living room. She watched her mother and father get into the car and drive away. She walked over to the table and picked up the letter. The letter arrived yesterday. Her father read it, and then gave it to her mother. They seemed shocked. They didn't talk to Rose about the letter. But Rose was interested. Why were her mother and father shocked?

She took the letter out of the envelope and looked at the Chinese letters. Rose and her family moved to the USA from Hong Kong when she was five years old. She went to Chinese school every Saturday morning for a few years, but she couldn't read Chinese very well. But she could understand some of the letter. Her grandmother in Hong Kong was very sick. She was dying. The letter was from a man called Mr Liu. Rose didn't know Mr Liu.

Maybe he is my father's friend, or my grandmother's friend, she thought. She put the letter down and closed her eyes. She had memories of her grandmother. When Rose was a child, her grandmother took her to the park and bought her ice cream. She was a kind woman. She sang songs to Rose, and told her stories. Rose started to cry.

I want to see my grandmother before she dies, she thought. *But I can't go back to Hong Kong. No one in my family can go back there. Not now...*

Rose put the letter back in the envelope and put it on the table. When Rose was a child, she often asked her mother and father, "Why did we leave Hong Kong? Why did we come to the USA?"

Her mother and father said, "We will tell you when you are older."

Then, when Rose was eighteen, her mother told her. A long time ago, Rose's father borrowed money from a gang. He wanted to start his own business. The business was not successful. He couldn't pay back the money to the gang. The leader of the gang was a bad man. He said to Rose's father, "If you don't pay back the money, we will kill you and your family." So, Rose's father took his family to the USA. Rose wanted to go back to Hong Kong, to see her grandmother and her home, but her mother said, "No. We can never go back. It's too dangerous."

Rose sat down on the sofa and switched her iPad on. She looked at pictures of Hong Kong.

I want to go back, she thought. *I want to see my grandmother. But if I ask my mother and father, they will say, 'no'. But I am twenty-four years old now. I am not a child. And the gang won't know me. I was five years old when I left Hong Kong.*

Then, she had an idea.

I will go to Hong Kong. I will see my grandmother. But I will say to my mother and father, 'I am going to New York to see my friends.'

She opened up a travel company website and started to look for flights from Los Angeles to Hong Kong. She found a cheap flight for one week later. She picked up her phone and called her boss at the bookstore where she worked. She said, "My grandmother is dying. I need to see her. Can I take a week off work?" Her boss said, "OK". She put her phone down and bought an aeroplane ticket.

CHAPTER TWO

Rose sat on the train. She was travelling from the airport into Hong Kong. She looked at her phone. In Mr Liu's letter, he wrote the name of her grandmother's hospital. Rose searched for it on Google. It was an expensive private hospital north of Kowloon. Rose found it on the map. It was small, but it had large gardens.

Rose was feeling tired. She wanted to sleep. She looked at the time. It was 8:00pm.

I'll eat something quickly, and then go to my hotel and sleep, she thought. *Then, tomorrow, I'll go to the hospital to see my grandmother.*

She thought about her mother and father. They were surprised when she said, "I'm going to New York," but they did not ask too many questions. Rose often travelled to different cities to see her friends.

If they know I am in Hong Kong, they will be very angry, she thought.

The train arrived at Kowloon Station, and Rose got off. She went out of the station and looked up at the dark sky.

Hong Kong. My home, she thought. *I'm home.*

She got into a taxi and gave the driver the name of her hotel. From the taxi window, she looked out at the tall buildings.

The city looks different, she thought. *Or maybe it looks the same...I can't remember very well. I was only a young child when I left here.*

The taxi stopped outside a hotel on Nathan Road. She paid the driver, and got out of the taxi. The driver helped her with her small suitcase. She looked around. There were still many people in the streets. There were many tourists and office workers, and many cars.

3

It was noisy.

This is very different from our home in our quiet street in LA, she thought. She went into the hotel.

Ten minutes later, after checking in and putting her suitcase in her room, she went out to find something to eat. She found a small restaurant and ate some noodles.

I remember this taste, she thought. *These noodles taste like the noodles my grandmother made.*

Rose thought about her grandmother. *When she sees me, will she know my face? Will she remember me? Will she be pleased to see me? I hope so.*

Rose finished her noodles and walked out into the street. It was a warm evening. She walked back to the hotel, went to her room, had a shower, and got into bed. She fell asleep very quickly.

CHAPTER THREE

On Hong Kong Island, David Liu was sitting in a small bar with two of his friends. One of his friends was called John. He was a gang member. The other friend was called Michelle. She was another gang member's girlfriend. She was a nurse in a private hospital. Rose's grandmother was in the same hospital.

"Do you think Chen will come to see his mother?" asked John.

David took a drink of beer. "I don't know," he said. "But if he comes, we are ready." John smiled. "What are you going to do if he comes back?"

"We are going to kill him," said David.

"Maybe his wife, or daughter will come back," said Michelle.

"If they come back, I'll kill them too," said David. "Chen took my money. I told him, 'If I see you or your family, I will kill you.' So he ran away to the US."

"But maybe Chen doesn't know his mother is sick," said Michelle. She was drinking champagne, and she felt a little drunk.

David looked at her. "Of course he knows! My father wrote him a letter! I told you that before!"

"Oh yes," said Michelle. "I forgot."

"My father is a friend of Chen's mother. That's why I never killed her. If I kill Chen's mother, my father will kill me. He married my mother, but I think he always loved Chen's mother. He wants her to see her family before she dies."

David looked at Michelle. "Has anyone visited her?"

"Only your father. If anyone else visits her, I will tell you," said

Michelle.

"If anyone visits her, call me on my phone. I don't want any of Chen's family to escape. I don't think his wife will come, but maybe his daughter will come. She was five when Chen took his family to the US."

He took his phone out of his pocket. "Her name is Rose. Look, she's on Instagram."

He opened up Instagram and showed Michelle some pictures of Rose.

"She is pretty," said Michelle.

"Yes, she is," said David. "But she will be prettier when she is dead."

John laughed. "Chen made a mistake when he took your money," he said.

"Oh yes," said David. "He made a big mistake twenty years ago, but now, his mother is dying. Maybe he will come back."

CHAPTER FOUR

Rose woke up and looked at the time. It was 7:00am.

I slept for nine hours, she thought. She sat up and stretched. She felt better. She got out of bed and opened the curtains. It was a bright, sunny day.

She had a quick shower and then went downstairs for breakfast. While she was eating breakfast and drinking coffee, she checked her email on her phone. There was a message from her mother.

--- *'I hope you are enjoying New York! Send us some pictures!'* ---

Oh no, thought Rose. *My mother wants me to send her pictures of New York! What can I do?*

Then, she had an idea.

--- *'The camera on my phone is not working very well. I think it's broken.'* --- she wrote.

I feel bad lying to my mother, but I can't tell her I am not in New York, she thought.

She finished breakfast and went back to her room. She opened her suitcase and took out a long orange dress. It was her favourite dress. She wanted to look nice when she met her grandmother. She put the dress on.

It will be hot today, so this dress is perfect, she thought. She took some photographs out of her bag. They were photographs of Rose with her grandmother. In the photographs, Rose and her grandmother were sitting in a park. They were smiling.

I was always so happy with my grandmother, thought Rose. *And she was so happy with me. I hope she will be happy to see me today.*

She put the photographs back in her bag and walked out of her hotel room. She took the elevator down to the lobby.

"Excuse me," she said to the man at the front desk. "I want to go to Primrose Hospital. It is here, in the New Territories." She showed the man the map on her phone. "What is the best way to get there?"

The man looked at the map. "You can take the Metro, and then a taxi," he said.

"Thank you," said Rose. She walked out of the hotel.

It's so hot out here! she thought. *I'm glad my dress is thin.*

She walked to the Metro and got on a train. The train had air conditioning and was cool. It was not so crowded. Rose began to feel nervous.

What will my grandmother say to me? she thought. *Can she speak? Maybe she is so ill that she cannot speak. I hope she can speak. I want to talk about our time together. I want to talk about my mother and father. I want to hear about her life in Hong Kong. I want to ask her so many questions!*

The train arrived at the station near the hospital, and Rose got off. Outside the station the air was hot. She found a taxi and asked the driver to take her to the hospital.

"That's an expensive hospital," said the driver. "Only rich people go there."

"My grandmother is there," said Rose.

"So you have a rich grandmother!" said the driver.

Is my grandmother rich? thought Rose. *My grandfather died before I was born. He was a cook. I'm sure they didn't have much money. I didn't think about this before. Why is she in an expensive hospital?*

"This is it," said the driver. He stopped the taxi. Rose looked out of the window. There were large metal gates, and high walls.

"How do I get in there?" asked Rose.

"I think there is an intercom. Press the button next to the gate and you can speak to someone."

"OK, thanks," said Rose. She paid the driver, and got out of the taxi. She found the button and pressed it. There was a camera.

"Yes?" said a woman's voice.

"I'm here to visit Zhou Lihua," said Rose.

There was no answer.

"Hello? Hello? I'm here to visit Zhou Lihua," said Rose again.

A few seconds later, the gate opened.

CHAPTER FIVE

Rose was surprised. There was a beautiful garden, with colourful flowers and trees. There was a small pond on the right. On her left, she saw an old man sitting on a bench. He was with a nurse. The man and the nurse watched Rose, but they didn't say anything. In front of her, there was a small building. It was white, and looked new. She walked towards the building.

The flowers smell nice, she thought. *The garden and the building are beautiful. I'm sure my grandmother is comfortable here.*

She opened the hospital door and went inside. There was a nurse standing next to a desk. She was waiting for Rose. She smiled. Another nurse was standing behind her. The first nurse said to the other nurse, "I'll talk to her." The other nurse looked worried. She didn't say anything.

"You can go," said the first nurse. The second nurse looked at Rose and walked into another room. The first nurse smiled at Rose again.

"Are you here to see Ms Zhou?" she asked.

"Yes, that's right."

"What's your name?" asked the nurse.

"I'm Rose Chen," said Rose.

The nurse looked at Rose for a few seconds, and then she smiled. "Ms Chen, please come with me."

Rose followed the nurse into a room. There was a table in the middle of the room, and there were four chairs. "Please sit down. Would you like a cup of tea?"

"Er, yes, thank you. But, I came here to see my grandmother. Can I see her?"

The nurse smiled. "I'll get some tea. Please wait here."

Rose had a bad feeling. "Is she dead?" asked Rose.

"No, she isn't," said the nurse. "Please. Wait."

The nurse went out of the room and closed the door. Rose looked around. The room was bright. The walls were white and there was a colourful painting on the wall.

Maybe this is the visitor's room, she thought. She put her bag on the chair next to her. She sat down and waited.

A few minutes later, the nurse came back. "Here is some tea," she said. She gave Rose a cup of tea and sat down.

Rose drank a little tea. *What kind of tea is this?* she thought. *It tastes strange.*

"Please. Drink the tea," said the nurse.

Rose didn't want to look rude, so she drank some more.

"So how is my grandmother? Can I see her?"

The nurse smiled. "Your grandmother is not well. She is having an operation now."

"An operation?" asked Rose. "What kind of operation? She is old. I don't think she can have an operation."

"Oh don't worry. It is not a big operation. Just a small operation. On her eye. She couldn't see very well."

"Oh," said Rose. "Can I see her tomorrow?"

"Yes, you can come back tomorrow. Please, drink your tea."

Rose felt sick. "I feel strange," she said. "Maybe I need some water."

This is strange, thought Rose. *I don't feel well. I should go.*

She stood up. She looked around the room. The room was moving. She picked up her bag and walked out of the room.

"What time will you come tomorrow?" asked the nurse.

"In the morning. About ten o'clock," said Rose. The light was very bright. It hurt her eyes. She walked to the gate. The nurse opened it. "See you tomorrow," she said. She closed the gate behind Rose.

"Hey, you!"

She looked up and saw two men. They were getting out of a car.

"Yes?" she said.

"We want to talk to you," said one of the men.

Rose had a bad feeling. She ran very quickly down a small street. Her head was hurting, but she ran fast. One of the men followed her. She ran down two more streets. She saw a small restaurant. She went inside.

"Please help me," she said to the owner. "A man is chasing me. Please let me hide here."

The owner was a woman. "Come here, into the kitchen," she said. Rose ran into the kitchen and sat down on a chair. She had a headache and she couldn't breathe very well. A few seconds later, a man came into the restaurant.

"Have you seen a young woman in an orange dress?" he asked the owner.

"No, I haven't," said the woman. "Would you like something to eat?"

"No," said the man. He walked out of the restaurant and ran down the road.

The woman walked into the kitchen. "Do you want me to call the police?" she asked.

"No thank you," said Rose. "But could I have a glass of water, please? I feel sick."

The woman gave her some water.

"Please let me stay here for a few minutes."

"No problem," said the woman.

Rose drank the cold water. She felt a little better. The woman started cooking.

"Could you call me a taxi please?" asked Rose.

"Of course. Where do you want to go?"

"To a hotel in Kowloon," said Rose.

CHAPTER SIX

David looked at John. They were sitting in David's apartment. It was a luxury apartment on the 30th floor of a high building. "She escaped? How?" asked David.

"She was too fast for us," said John. He felt nervous. David was angry.

"But Michelle put drugs in her tea! How could she run so quickly?"

"Maybe the drugs weren't strong enough," said John.

David hit the coffee table. He took a cigarette and lit it.

"I don't believe it. How can a young woman run faster than you?"

"I don't know. I'm sorry," said John. "But I have good news from Michelle."

"What's that?" asked David.

"Rose is going to go to the hospital tomorrow at ten o'clock. We can catch her then. If she doesn't go to the police."

David laughed. "She won't go to the police. She can't. When her father was in Hong Kong, he did bad things. He borrowed money from bad people. He borrowed money from us, and also from other people. If she goes to the police, her father will have trouble. And she will be worried about her grandmother. If she goes to the police, her grandmother might be in danger. No, I don't think she will go to the police."

"So what is the plan?" asked John.

"We catch her at the hospital tomorrow morning. We bring her back here. We tell her to call her father. She will say to her father,

12

'Send a million dollars, or the gang will kill me. If you call the police, the gang will kill me.' Then, we keep her here until her father sends the money," said David.

"But does her father have a million dollars?" asked John.

"I don't know," said David. "But he can borrow it. If he doesn't give us the money, we will kill his daughter. So, I think he will find the money."

John laughed. "Good plan. I like it."

CHAPTER SEVEN

The next morning, Rose got up early. She sat on her bed and thought about the day before.

Were those men waiting for me outside the hospital? she thought. *Who were they? They knew I was in the hospital. How did they know that? Maybe they were not waiting for me. The hospital is an expensive one. I'm sure many of the visitors are rich. Maybe they wanted to steal money from me. Maybe they wait for visitors to come out, and then they try to take their money. I have to be careful.*

She looked out of the window. It was still early, but there were people going to work. Rose saw a man. He was standing across the road. He was looking at the hotel.

Who is he? she thought. *Maybe he is waiting for someone.*

Rose put on a blue dress and went to the hotel restaurant to have breakfast. Thirty minutes later, she went back to her room. She looked out of the window.

That man is still here! That is strange. Is he watching the hotel?

Rose felt nervous. *Is he waiting for me? It is still early, so I will wait an hour before I go to the hospital.*

Rose sat on the bed and switched the TV on. She watched the news for an hour, then she switched the TV off. She looked out of the window again.

The man is still here! I don't like this. Maybe he is waiting for me. How can I get out of the hotel? If I go out of the front doors, he will see me. Maybe the hotel has a back door.

Rose picked up her bag and walked out of the room. She walked down the stairs of the hotel. She went into the lobby. There were many people in the lobby. The man on the front desk was busy. Rose saw a door. There was a sign on the door – "Staff only". Rose opened the door and walked into the room. It was a store room. There were many cleaning items in the room. There was also another door. She opened the door, and she was outside, in a yard.

"Excuse me!"

She turned around. There was a man wearing a chef's uniform. He was walking towards her.

"Excuse me. You can't use this door. This is for staff only," said the man.

"Sorry," said Rose. "I made a mistake." She walked quickly to the gate and walked out of the yard.

She walked down a narrow path, and then onto a small street. She walked away from the main road.

She looked at a map on her phone.

It will take a long time, but I can get to the station this way, she thought. *The man outside the hotel won't see me.*

Rose walked quickly. After about twenty minutes, she arrived at the station. She looked around. No one was watching her. A few minutes later, she was on the train. She looked around the train. She couldn't see the man.

Maybe he wasn't waiting for me, she thought. *Maybe I am too nervous.*

She got off the train at the stop near the hospital and got into a taxi. The taxi took her to the hospital. She paid the driver and got out. She pressed the button and waited. After a few seconds, a voice said, "Hello?"

"Hello, my name is Rose Chen. I came yesterday to see my grandmother, Zhou Lihua. Can I see her today?"

"Of course. Please come in," said the voice.

The gate unlocked and Rose opened it. She walked through the garden to the building.

"Good morning, Rose," said the nurse.

"Good morning. I'm sorry about yesterday. I left quickly. I felt sick."

The nurse smiled. "That's OK. Many people feel sick when they go into hospitals. Please wait in this room."

She took Rose into the visitor's room.

"Your grandmother is having a wash. Please wait here for a few minutes."

Rose sat down and the nurse went out of the room and closed the door.

A few minutes later, the door opened. The nurse came into the room. There were two men behind her. Rose looked at the men.

"You were in the car yesterday! You were waiting for me!" she said. She stood up.

One of the men took a gun out of his jacket.

"Be quiet, or I will kill you," he said quietly.

"What?" Rose was shocked. She looked at the nurse. The nurse smiled. "Be quiet," she said.

"But...but...wait!" Rose tried to speak, but the other man held her arm. "Follow us. If you shout for help, we will kill you. Get out."

The men took Rose out of the room. Rose saw another nurse.

I saw her yesterday, she thought. *Maybe she will help me. Maybe she will call the police.*

"Help!" said Rose.

"She won't help you," said the man with the gun. "If she says anything, or goes to the police, we will kill her too!"

The men took Rose out into the garden. The first nurse was smiling.

"Good work, Michelle," said one of the men.

"I'm glad I could help," said Michelle. "Goodbye Rose."

"Who are you? What are you doing? Why are you doing this?" asked Rose.

One of the men opened the gate, and the other one pushed her into a car. The men got in the car and locked the doors.

"If you try to escape, we will kill you," said the man with the gun. "Close your eyes." Rose closed her eyes. The other man was driving. He drove very quickly.

After about forty minutes, the car stopped.

"Open your eyes," said the man with the gun. Rose opened her eyes. They were in an underground car park.

"Get out of the car. Don't say anything. Don't try to run away."

Rose and the men got out of the car. They walked into an elevator. One of the men pressed a button and the elevator moved. A few seconds later, the elevator stopped.

"Get out," said the man with the gun. They walked out of the elevator.

This is an apartment building, thought Rose. *It looks expensive.*

They stopped outside a door and the door opened. The man with the gun pushed Rose inside.

A man was in the apartment. He smiled at Rose.

"Welcome," he said. "Follow me." Rose walked through the apartment to a living room. She looked around. There were big windows with views of the city. There were large sofas and a big TV. There were paintings on the walls.

The owner of this apartment is rich, thought Rose.

"Sit down," said the man. Rose sat down.

CHAPTER EIGHT

"Who are you? What do you want?" asked Rose. The men smiled.

"Who are we? We are friends of your father," said one of the men. The other men laughed. "I am David. But you can call me Mr Liu."

"Liu?" Rose thought about the letter in her house in the US. "Did you write a letter to my father?"

David looked angry. "No. My father wrote it. But let's not talk about my father. Let's talk about your father."

"What about my father?" asked Rose.

"A long time ago, your father borrowed some money from me. He didn't pay me back. So, he took you and his wife to the United States. Do you know about that?"

"My mother told me some things about my father and money," said Rose. "But, what do you want me to do? I can't pay you."

The man smiled. It was not a nice smile. "I understand. You can't pay us. But your father can pay us. If he pays us, you can live. If he doesn't pay us, you will die."

"What? But, you can't kill me!" Rose wanted to cry.

"Of course we can kill you," said David. "I've killed other people. Why can't I kill you?"

"But, but...I was only a child when my father took me to the United States. I am not a bad person!" said Rose.

"No, you are not a bad person. Maybe I will feel bad when I kill you."

"Don't kill me! Please!" shouted Rose.

"If you don't want to die, call your father now. Say to him 'send a million dollars, or I will die.'"

"A million dollars? But my father is not a rich man! He doesn't have a million dollars!"

"He can borrow it. If he doesn't, his daughter will die." David stood up and walked over to a table. He picked up the phone and gave it to Rose.

"Call him. Now."

Rose took the phone from David. Her hands were shaking. She pressed the numbers of her family phone number and waited.

"Hello?"

When Rose heard her father's voice, she started to cry.

"Dad? It's me, Rose."

"Rose! Are you OK? What's wrong?"

"Dad, I'm so sorry. I'm in Hong Kong."

"What?"

"I'm in Hong Kong. I read the letter about my grandmother. I wanted to see her. So I came to Hong Kong..."

"I don't believe it! Get out of Hong Kong now! Come home! There are dangerous people there!"

"I can't come home. I'm with a group of men. I'm with a man called David Liu."

"David Liu? I have to call the police. This is terrible!"

"Don't call the police, Dad. David will kill me if you call the police. And he will kill me if you don't send him a million dollars!"

"Give me the phone!" said David.

"Good evening Mr Chen. It's your old friend David. Do you understand? A million dollars, in the next forty-eight hours, or we kill your daughter! If you go to the police, we will kill her."

Rose watched David. He looked angry. "You can get the money in Hong Kong? OK. We will wait for you here. We will keep your daughter here until you come and give us the money....what? You want three days? No. Forty-eight hours. Or she dies!" David hung up the phone. He looked at Rose.

"So, your father said, 'I will come to Hong Kong and give you the money. But let my daughter go.' Of course, we will not let you go. You will stay here, until your father gives us the money."

He walked over to the table and put the phone back. "So, relax. You are going to stay with me for a few days. You can't escape. This is the thirtieth floor of the building. If you try to jump from the balcony, you will die. The door is locked, so you can't escape out of the front door. If you go near the door, we will kill you. So, what would you like to do? Watch TV?"

David switched the TV on.

"I'm going to talk to my men in the next room. Don't move!"

David and the men stood up and walked out and went into the next room.

Rose thought about her father.

He will be very angry with me, she thought. *Maybe my father will die. Or maybe I will die. It was a bad idea to come to Hong Kong. But I want to see my grandmother. I came to see her. Why is that so bad?*

CHAPTER NINE

Rose looked around the room.

I have to escape, she thought. *But how can I escape?*

She stood up and went to the window. There was a small balcony outside the window.

I am thirty floors above the ground. I can't escape from the balcony! She looked to the side. The next apartment's balcony was very near. *Can I climb over to that balcony?* She looked down at the city below, and she felt sick. *It is dangerous, but I have to try something. But if David and the other men see me, they will kill me. But if I don't escape, they will kill my father. I have to do this.*

She picked up her bag and put it around her neck. Very slowly, Rose opened the large window. The wind was not so strong. She stepped out onto the balcony and looked down. *What am I doing?* she thought. *Are there any people in the next apartment? Are they friends of David? This is a risk, but I have to do this.*

Very carefully, she put her legs over the balcony railing so she was sitting on the railing. *Don't look down, Rose,* she thought. *Don't look down.*

She reached across to the next balcony with her arms. She touched the railings of the next balcony and jumped. She tried to put her feet on the balcony railing, but she slipped. She was holding onto the balcony railing with just her hands.

Oh no! she thought. *I can't hold onto the railings! I'm going to fall!*

Then, a woman in the next apartment looked out of the window. She looked very shocked. She opened the window.

"Who are you? What are you doing?" she asked.

"Help me! Please! Help me! I'm going to fall!" said Rose.

The woman walked out onto the balcony and held Rose's arms. She pulled very hard. Rose put one of her feet on the bottom railing of the balcony and the woman pulled her again. Soon, Rose was standing on the balcony.

"Thank you so much," she said. "Please, you have to help me. The man in the next apartment wants to kill me!"

"I don't know the man in the next apartment, but I heard he is a dangerous man. Come with me. You can escape from my apartment."

"Thank you so much," said Rose. "If you see the man in the next apartment, please don't tell him about me."

"I won't tell him. Don't worry. He won't trouble me. My husband is a top gang member in the city. Now, go! Quickly!"

Rose ran to the front door and went out quietly. She got in the elevator and went down to the ground floor. She ran through the streets until she found a small park. She sat on a bench and called her father.

"Dad? It's me. I escaped," she said.

"You escaped? Good! Go to the airport now! Take the next flight to LA. You have to come quickly. If you don't, they will kill you!"

"Will you come to Hong Kong?"

"If you can come back to LA, no I won't. But if they catch you, I will. And they will kill us both! Hurry!"

"But my suitcase is in my hotel!"

"Forget your suitcase! Do you have your passport and money? Or your credit card?"

"Yes, they are in my bag."

"So go to the airport. Get a flight out of Hong Kong now!"

Rose hung up and ran to the nearest station. She found a taxi.

She got in the taxi and said to the driver, "To the airport please. And drive fast!"

CHAPTER TEN

Lihua Zhou was lying in a hospital bed in a large private room. She looked at the nurse.

"A young woman came to see me?" she asked. She spoke slowly. She was very weak.

The nurse smiled. "Yes. She was around twenty-four years old. She came to see you, but Michelle took her into the visitor's room. Then, two men came. I couldn't call the police. If I call the police, the men will kill me."

Lihua tried to sit up.

"Please. Lie down," said the nurse. "You are very sick."

"No," said Lihua. Slowly, she sat up. "I need to call someone. Bring me a phone."

The nurse was worried, but she went out of the room. A few minutes later, she returned with a phone.

"I can't see very well. Can you call this number?" Lihua told the nurse a telephone number and the nurse called it.

"Here you are," said the nurse. She gave the phone to Lihua. A man answered the phone.

"Guotai, it's me," said Lihua. "I need your help. My granddaughter came to see me....yes....Rose...no, I didn't see her. Some men came. They took her....OK....thank you."

Lihua gave the phone back to the nurse.

"Was that your friend, Mr Liu?" asked the nurse.

Lihua smiled. "Yes, it was. He will help us. He knows the men."

"How does he know the men?" asked the nurse.

"One of the men is his son," said Lihua. She looked sad. "My son borrowed money from him twenty years ago. He couldn't pay the money back, and he was in trouble. David, my friend's son, wanted to kill him. My son took his family to the United States. They have never come back to Hong Kong. David was a nice boy when he was a child. But when he was eighteen, he joined a gang. He has done many bad things. But he is scared of his father."

"Mr Liu is a good friend to you," said the nurse. "He visits you very often."

Lihua smiled. "A long time ago, we were very good friends. He wanted to marry me! But I had to marry another man. My father chose my husband. But..." Lihua looked at the nurse. "I always loved him. And he always loved me."

CHAPTER ELEVEN

"Who is that?" David said. He was sitting with John and the other man in the room next to the living room. He walked into the hall and looked at the screen on the wall.

"It's my father," he said. Just then, his phone rang.

"Don't answer it!" shouted John.

"I have to answer it! My father will be angry!" said David. "Hello?"

"I know you are in your apartment. Open the door," said Guotai.

"I'm not in my apartment," said David.

"Yes, you are! I asked the apartment manager. He said, 'David's car is in the car park.' So open the door!"

David hung up and pressed the button to open the door. He walked back into the room.

"My father is coming in," he said. "He probably wants to talk about money. I will bring him into this room, not the living room. Rose is still in the living room."

A few seconds later, Guotai knocked on the door. David opened it. Guotai didn't say anything. He walked into the apartment.

"Where is she?" he asked.

David looked surprised. "Who?"

"You know who!" said Guotai. "Rose! Where is Rose?"

"I don't know…who is Rose?"

Guotai pushed David and walked to the living room.

"No!" shouted David.

Guotai opened the living room door and walked inside. David

walked into the living room too.

"What?" he said. "John, George, come here! She's gone!"

"Who has gone?" asked Guotai. He pushed his son again. "Tell me! If you don't tell me, I will call the police!"

"OK, OK, I'll tell you. We found Rose Chen at the hospital. We brought her here. She was in the living room. But she has gone."

"Where has she gone?" asked Guotai.

David and Guotai walked to the window.

"The window is open!" said David. "But she can't jump from here! It is too high! But the front door was locked. She couldn't go out of the front door. I don't understand…"

"Maybe the person in the next apartment helped her to climb to the next apartment," said John.

"What was she wearing?" asked Guotai.

"A blue dress," said David.

Guotai looked at David. "I know you are my son, but if you try to find her, I'll kill you!" He walked out of the apartment and got into the elevator.

The airport, he thought. *I have to go to the airport. But first, I have to call the hospital. I hope the nurse can help me.*

CHAPTER TWELVE

Rose was in the airport. She went to the check-in desk.

"I changed my return flight," she said to the woman on the check-in desk. "I will go back to the US today."

"OK," said the woman. "Do you have any baggage?"

"No," said Rose. "I lost it."

"Rose! Rose! Rose Chen!"

Rose turned around. An old man was standing in the centre of the airport. He was shouting her name.

The woman looked at her passport. "He is looking for you," she said.

"It's Guotai Liu! I'm a friend of your grandmother!" shouted the man. People were looking at him.

Liu! thought Rose. *He wrote the letter to my father!*

"Please wait," she said to the woman on the check-in desk. She walked over to Guotai.

"I'm Rose Chen," she said.

Guotai looked at her and smiled.

"Rose! I'm your grandmother's friend. I wrote a letter to your father about your grandmother."

"But how did you find me?"

Guotai shook his head. "We have no time to talk. We must go back to Hong Kong."

"Back to Hong Kong? I can't go back to Hong Kong. Bad men are trying to kill me!"

"No, they are not. One of the bad men is my son. I said to him,

'If you try to find Rose, I will kill you!' So, he won't try to find you. Come on, we have to hurry!"

"Where are we going?" asked Rose.

"You'll see," said Guotai. He took her hand and they walked out of the airport quickly.

Rose and Guotai got into his car. It was a big, luxury car.

This man is rich, thought Rose. Guotai drove very quickly.

"Do you know my father?" asked Rose.

"Yes, I know your father. He was friends with my son at school. But then, he borrowed money from my son. My son became bad. He lends people money. If they cannot pay back the money, he kills them. Your father borrowed money from my son, but he couldn't pay him back. So, my son wanted to kill him. Your father took you and his wife to the United States. You are safe there."

"Why didn't he kill my grandmother?"

Guotai smiled. "Because your grandmother is my friend. My special friend. If he does a bad thing to your grandmother, of course, I will kill him."

"But he is your son! You can't kill your son!"

"Yes, he is my son, but your grandmother is more important to me than him."

Thirty minutes later, the car stopped outside the hospital.

"The hospital!" said Rose. "My grandmother!"

"Yes, you are going to see your grandmother!" said Guotai. "Come on."

They got out of the car.

"But the nurse…she is bad…"

"The bad nurse is not working today. Don't worry."

Guotai pressed the button and the gate opened. They walked through the garden to the building. The nurse was waiting for them.

"Follow me," she said.

They followed her. The nurse stopped outside a room. She knocked.

"Come in," said a small voice.

The nurse opened the door and Rose and Guotai went inside.

"Grandmother!" said Rose. She walked to the bed and took her grandmother's hand.

Lihua smiled. "Rose! My dear Rose! I've missed you!" she said. "You were only five years old. Now, you are a beautiful young woman!"

Rose sat down next to the bed and started to cry.

"We will give you time alone," said Guotai. He and the nurse walked out of the room and closed the door.

CHAPTER THIRTEEN

Rose looked at her mother and father. They were sitting in the living room in their house. She arrived back in the US a few hours earlier.

"I know you are angry with me," she said. "But I wanted to see my grandmother. I love her very much."

Her father smiled. "Of course we were angry. I was very angry. But, now, I'm glad you went to see my mother."

"Are you?" asked Rose.

"Yes, I am. I called the hospital in Hong Kong. Your grandmother died at the time you left Hong Kong. I'm glad she could see a family member before she died," said her father. "I'm sure she was lonely. She lived without her family for twenty years. But she saw you. The nurse at the hospital said, 'That was her last wish. To see her granddaughter.'"

Rose started to cry. "I did a dangerous thing. I'm sorry. You were worried about me. But," she looked at her mother and father. "I'm glad I went. But I promise. I won't do anything dangerous again!"

THANK YOU

Thank you for reading Hunted in Hong Kong. (Word count: 7,276) We hope you enjoyed it. Other books in the City Thriller series are Trouble in Paris, Danger in Seattle, and Adventure in Rome.

There are quizzes about this book on our free study site I Talk You Talk Press EXTRA. http://italk-youtalk.com

If you would like to read more graded readers, please visit our website http://www.italkyoutalk.com

Other Level 2 graded readers include
Adventure in Rome
Andre's Dream
A Passion for Music
Christmas Tales
Danger in Seattle
Don't Come Back
Finders Keepers…
Marcy's Bakery
Men's Konkatsu Tales
Salaryman Secrets!
Stories for Halloween
The Perfect Wedding
The House in the Forest
The School on Bolt Street

Train Travel
Trouble in Paris
Women's Konkatsu Tales

ABOUT THE AUTHOR

I Talk You Talk Press is a Japan-based publisher of language textbooks, graded readers and language learning/teaching resources.

Our team is made up of highly experienced language teachers and translators, who have all studied at least one additional language to an advanced level.

This experience enables us to design our materials from the perspective of both the teacher and the learner. We consult with both teachers and language learners when designing our textbooks and graded readers, and test our materials extensively in the classroom before publication.

We are a fast-growing press, and currently publish graded readers for learners of English. We publish new graded readers monthly.

www.ingramcontent.com/pod-product-compliance
Lightning Source LLC
Chambersburg PA
CBHW022349040426
42449CB00006B/794